The Pile
Weaves

The Pile Weaves

Twenty-six Techniques
and how to do them

Jean Wilson

VNR VAN NOSTRAND REINHOLD COMPANY
New York   Cincinnati   Toronto   London   Melbourne

Dedication
To the first weaver who found a way to
simulate animal pelt

The author and Van Nostrand Reinhold Company
have taken all possible care to trace the
ownership of every work of art reproduced in
this book and to make full acknowledgment for
its use. If any errors have accidently
occurred, they will be corrected in subsequent
editions, providing notification is sent to
the publisher.

Books by Jean Wilson
Weaving You Can Wear
The Pile Weaves
Weaving is Creative
Weaving is Fun
Weaving is for Anyone

Van Nostrand Reinhold Company Regional Offices:
New York Cincinnati Chicago Millbrae Dallas
Van Nostrand Reinhold Company
International Offices:
London Toronto Melbourne

Library of Congress Catalog Card
Number: 72-2665
ISBN 0 442 29519 7 cl.
ISBN 0 442 29520 0 pb.

Designed by Rod Josey
Printed in England by Jolly & Barber Ltd, Rugby
and bound by Henry Brooks, Cowley, Oxford

Published in 1974 by Van Nostrand Reinhold
Company, a Division of Litton Educational
Publishing, Inc.
450 West 33rd Street, New York, N.Y. 10001
and by Van Nostrand Reinhold Company Limited,
25-28 Buckingham Gate, London SW1E 6LQ

16 15 14 13 12 11 10 9 8 7 6 5 4 3 2 1

*C-1. Wall hanging, a
composition of pile weaves.
Top and bottom bands are
Greek Soumak. Outlines are
vertical Soumak. Other
techniques included are
Boutonné, Eigg, Ghiordes
Knot (cut and loops),
Icelandic, Czech, Egyptian,
Chivas, Highland Guatemalan,
along with plain weave and
overlay.*

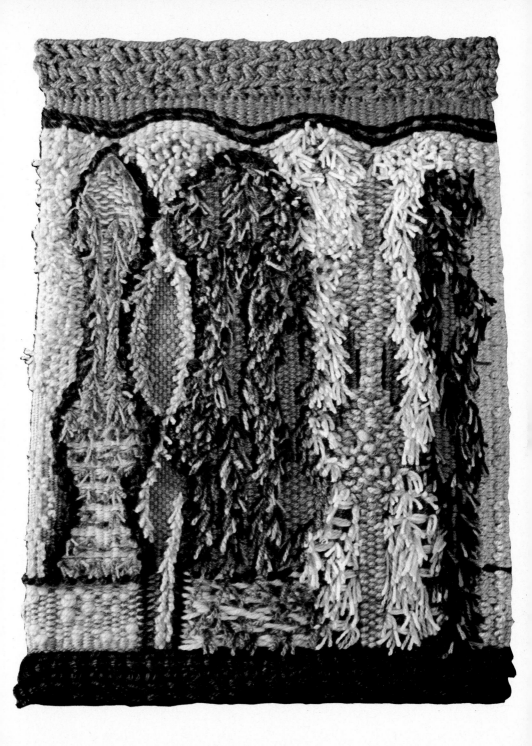

Contents

Color Illustrations page

All woven examples are by the author unless otherwise credited.
All drawings are by Gary Wilson.
All photographs are by Kent Kammerer unless otherwise credited.

A★

Acknowledgments

Once more, my grateful thanks to Kent Kammerer for his excellent photographs, and for the time he spent on the special effects;
A heart-felt thank-you to my son, Gary Wilson, who so ably drew the working drawings for me;
Special thanks to Nancy Newman, senior editor Van Nostrand Reinhold, for her ready cooperation and enthusiasm;
Warm thanks to Margaret Holton, again my skilful editor, for her sustained interest;
And to everyone mentioned in the captions — my appreciation for interest and help.

jean wilson

Part I
Pile Weave Preliminaries

Pile Weave Defined

Pile weaves have ends of yarn, cut or looped, rising above a flat background weave to create surface interest (figure 1-1). Technically, this is a compound weave that has a basic weft woven as the ground, plus a supplementary weft that forms the pile or raised surface. The pile yarns are an addition to the ground weave

1-1. This is Pile Weave.

1-2. Wool pile, richly carved into facets. Designer-craftsman Fritzi Oxley. Shown in color on page 16. (Photographed by Beverly Rush.)

Right. 1-3. Rya rug, Ghiordes Knot. (Photograph courtesy the Henry Gallery, University of Washington.)

— they are an integral part of the weave. Surface texture is created by bringing these yarns up from the ground weave. The foundation weave can be completely covered, or the surface textures (pile) can be placed in small isolated areas or units of design. The pile surface can be shaggy, tightly-packed and upright, smoothed down in regular rows, or a wild, non-directional tangle of cut ends. It can be composed of high or low loops, or a combination of cut and uncut loops. When tightly packed in it can be carved or shaped into surface patterns (figure 1-2). Woven pile weaves are made with pre-cut wefts, continuous weft in shuttle or hand bobbins, or needle stitches put in as the weaving progresses.

We consider some of the wrapped weaves as surface interest — a raised surface added to a flat-weave ground, which puts them within the definition of a pile weave.

Pile fabric is much more than the usual image of the deep cut-pile Scandinavian-style rug, or velvet and corduroy, or commercially woven rugs and carpets, shags and loops. In this text we include more than two dozen techniques that create a raised surface through a large selection of methods. Wrapped, pulled-up, knotted, embroidery stitches, chaining, all serve to add another dimension to a flat background fabric.

1-4. Pine in Snow

1-5. Weaving related to "Pine in Snow."

1-6. Tapestry employing woven loops, seed pods, exotic bits of Hawaiian flora, and heavy yarns. Artist-weaver Ruthadell Anderson, for the Honolulu Academy of Arts. One of three sections. (Photograph by Raymond M. Sato.)

C-2. Diamonds in the Rough.
Carved pile by Fritzi Oxley.
(Photograph by Beverly
Rush.)

Everywhere in nature examples for pile weaves are abundant: thick pile in branches of pine and fir trees, with the additional texture of cones; tree branches with smaller twigs and branches forming casual, spaced pile; grass, weeds, a stand of Scotch broom; reeds growing in water; feathers on birds, hair and fur on animals — including humans. The silk of a milkweed pod going to seed — and the dandelion's golden crown, expanding into a white halo. Caterpillars, moss, waves, the instantly changing texture of raindrops in puddles, fluffy clouds — truly a boundless variety of surface textures surrounds us; they all fit the definition of a pile surface and provide constant inspiration for translation into pile weaves. (See figures 2-29–2-38 in Part II.)

Uses

Pile weaves are endlessly useful and such fun to work with. They are the exclamation points in a flat weave. They add a raised dimension to an otherwise smooth surface. They add warmth and weight where desirable. They display colors excitingly in any combination to create a whole new color effect. Note the differences in color shading in cut and uncut yarns; use this in your subtle designing. To sum up . . .
• Pile weaves for warmth, for added texture and dimension, for strength and wearing quality, for design.
• Pile weaves for the pleasure of weaving — the excitement of seeing a pattern emerge and develop in a raised surface.
• Pile weaves for the color blending; the play of deep textures against flat weaving — or open spaces.

The many methods

Given a warp, a selection of yarns — and lots of time — any weaver could "invent" a good many ways to achieve a pile surface. Most weavers limit themselves to the familiar picked-up loops and the Ghiordes Knot. This knot is so secure, allows for so much latitude in color change and patterns, that it truly is about the most useful one. It well earns the firm and historically important place it holds in pile weave methods. But for a change — try some others, described later.

The good Ghiordes Knot – and others

The Ghiordes (Oriental, Turkish, Flossa, Rya, etc.) is probably the most familiar and most-used pile knot. It appears everywhere in the world. It is rhythmic and pleasant to do, results are attractive, hold fast, and are durable. However, delving into archeological journals, out-of-print ethnic books, and with much experimentation and observation of pile weaves in nature, we found diverse other means to create a pile weave, each one adding something to the joy of learning new ways. Some methods employ cut ends, some are in loops. The choice is yours — and it is a wide one. Work with cut pieces of yarn, thrums, or from a bobbin or spool of continuous weft. Methods range from inches-long cut pile, to the merest raising of a weft into tiny loops; from the

1-7. Ghiordes Knot being
woven over a gauge.

18

securely wrapped-and-tied to a loose laying-in of extra wefts in an open weave, to be finished by washing and felting. There is a method and depth for any textile use. These weaves in such abundance serve to combine with and enhance any flat weave where shadow-play and surface interest is desired.

Types of Pile Weaves

Types of pile weaves are put into two main categories in this text.

Knotted or wrapped. This group includes those that use cut or continuous lengths of yarn put around the warp in a wrap or knot.

Woven pile. This category is where pile weft is woven into the shed, then picked up in loops, or the cut ends are laid in to form a cut pile; also woven overshot patterns, with long surface floats, which are cut. In addition, we look at some of the lofty embroidery stitches, which add a raised surface. These can be worked as you weave, or added to the fabric after removal from the loom.

A glossary of methods presented in Part II

Knotted and/or wrapped

Ghiordes Knot. Cut or loops. Variations, including the ends pulled out in loops.
Tibetan Rug Knot. Loops made over a gauge, usually cut.
Slip Loop. Pile weft is wrapped around warp, then pulled out in a loop. Something like the Tibetan Rug Knot, but no gauge is used.
Sehna (Persian) Rug Knot. Right-hand and left-hand. Cut ends.
Single Warp Spanish Knot. Cut ends, around just one warp.
Ancient (Old French, Middle Ages). Over one warp, cut ends. A bit more secure than the Single Warp Spanish.
Icelandic Pile. One end of weft is wrapped around warp. Cut ends. Ground weave is diagonal twill.
Egyptian Cut Pile. Traditionally woven with slub linen on a two/two basket weave ground. Cut ends laid in and wrapped.
Granitos. (Spanish Confite). Wefts wrapped around the warp to make two offset, low loops.
Oriental Soumak. We suggest it as a surface texture. It can be definite enough to become almost a loop. At one point, a loop can be pulled out.
Greek Soumak. By making many knots on one warp instead of the traditional three, and/or using thick or multiple wefts, this is a raised surface.

Chaining. A surface technique which can be loose and heavy for a rounded ridge. Weft may be chained in the air, then returned to the shed and caught in, leaving a raised line or mound.
Twining. Not in itself a pile weave, but it is a good foundation to hold feathers, tags of wool, loops, and so on.

1-8. A composition of pillows.
Techniques include Ghiordes
Knot, Oriental Soumak,
Egyptian Cut Pile, warp-ends
fastened to surface, Algerian
Eye Stitch, Highland
Guatemalan, Greek Soumak,
weft-ends tied, Ghiordes
Knot with plain weave.

C-3. **Lopi.** The pelt and the
wool of Iceland mountain
sheep.

C-4. Ghiordes Knot in all
directions, with a strip of
Icelandic sheepskin.

C-3

C-4

21

Woven Pile

Eigg. Cut ends laid in.

Highland Guatemalan Cut Pile. Similar to Eigg, but cut ends are placed in different order.

Czech Shepherd's Cloak Pile. A windblown shag weave, cut ends laid in.

Picked-up Loops. No wrapping or knotting — the pattern weft is woven into the shed and loops are raised up to the surface. A good many variations, including Chivas, Boutonné and Twisted Loops.

Chivas. A Guatemalan version of picked-up loops, with two wefts woven in each shed. Double loops separate, making a full surface.

Boutonné. A French-Canadian method with distinctive regional designs. Like a running stitch punctuated by round little loops that form geometric designs.

Twisted Loops. As each loop is pulled up, it is twisted. A more casual look than the regular loops pulled up, and a little more securely held.

Loom-controlled Pile Weaves

Thread your loom with an overshot pattern. Choose one with long surface-weft floats — they can be clipped into a short pile, scattered, or bordering the woven pattern. Some of these traditional patterns have weft floats on both sides, and can be used for a two-faced pile fabric. Two of the weaves that work well are Corduroy and Swivel, on pages 75-6. (See figures 2-22, -23, -24.)

Needlemade Pile Stitches

Some embroidery stitches are worked almost entirely on the surface and can be used to give texture to a plain weave or be added to a woven-pile technique. They can be worked while the cloth is woven, or after the piece is taken from the loom. We explore just a few — there are many possibilities.

Natural Pile

Fur as a source of design, and weaving with fur, which makes the pile surface. Design sources and materials in nature.

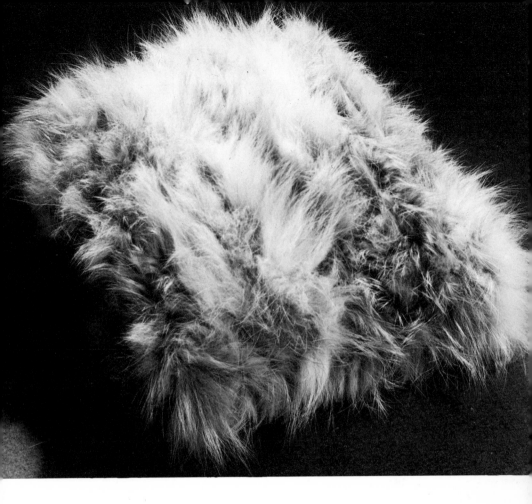

General information about weaving raised surfaces

For more extensive discussions — stories, history, variations, and
such — please refer to my three previous books, *Weaving is for
Anyone, Weaving is Fun*, and *Weaving is Creative*. Pile weaves
have been included in all of them.

When you plan to weave a pile surface, the following brief
notes will be helpful. Most apply to all the methods — loop or cut-
pile, worked over a gauge with continuous weft, with cut wefts or
picked-up loops. Special points pertaining to a specific type are
covered in Part II, with the directions. Each technique has as
many variations as there are weavers doing it. The warp sett, size
and kind of yarns for warp and weft, gauges used, scale, use of
the weaving, color, imagination of the weaver-designer — all

B

these can be applied to make limitless combinations and variations. We bring you the classic techniques — and you take it from there and make the techniques your own.

Generally speaking, any pile weave must be carefully woven to insure that the supplementary wefts will stay in place and do the job meant for them, that is, provide a raised surface and extra dimension to a flat-weave background. The knotted and wrapped weaves — such as the Ghiordes and Egyptian Cut Pile — are quite secure, in that they are put around the warps. The picked-up loops, laid-in pile weaves, and woven overshot patterns depend upon a closely-beaten background to hold them in place. Plan your weaving carefully to insure that your number of warps per inch, your weft ground weave, and the pile wefts work together to accomplish what you expect of them. For instance, a slick, smooth yarn should not be expected to produce a satisfactory picked-up loop fabric. The loops will slip, the beat will not be as close. For a wrapped pile weave a crisp yarn such as jute will not bend and cling as well as the softer wool. Cotton and wool will usually mat and shrink enough with washing to help secure loops or laid-in pile on textiles made for hard use.

Important to note

The following comments apply to all pile weaves. They are important points in the weaving of fabrics with a raised surface. After the proper planning, choice of loom, yarns, sett, and method, remember:

• Beat firmly. Beat before and after insertion of pile weft. Beat on an open and closed shed.

• Beat with a pulling, squeezing motion rather than a short, sharp beat. Ease the row into the preceding one.

• When using a fork or small beater, use the same easing, pressing motion.

• Always weave at least a row or two of ground before and after each pile row. This is necessary to keep the weft in place, support and firm it.

• Always fill in by weaving short rows at the selvedge when the ground weave with the regular number of rows does not fill in properly.

• After several rows are finished, go back and gently tug up or down on the pile to settle it in place and elevate it, particularly on a rug, so your rows are tight and the ground is full. Push ground wefts in with the fingers, too.

• Pile lengths are variable, weaver's choice, and can be just long enough to hold or very long and shaggy.

• All the laid-in and wrapped-and-knotted methods allow the weaver full scope for color. Many wefts can be combined and used as one; the techniques permit starting and stopping a color at any point in the weaving.

• Most of the pile techniques can be made to curve, either by gradually stepping the succeeding rows up and over, or by actually modelling and pushing them into curves, horizontally. Elliptical, round, wavy, ovals — there is a way to do it. (See C-5 on color page 40.) Weaving directions often sound involved, and at times very nearly impossible, but give them a try and you will find that your hands work together — and do them. The pile wefts and the ground wefts work together to hold all fast.

Supporting the raised surface

Always weave a heading at the beginning, and at end. An inch or more is usually sufficient to protect the main weaving. Weave more for a turned-back hem. Woven rows can be taken out and warps knotted or fastened in some manner to keep the fabric from ravelling. (See End Finishes page 90.)

Before and after each row of pile weave, always put in at least one row — preferably more — of ground weave. This helps to support the raised surface and keep it in place. It is mandatory to have firm rows before and after the picked-up loops, because these rows are important to keep the loops in, and standing. The ground-weave yarn can be very fine; it will disappear and tuck into the row of pile. Several rows may pack in and around the extra wefts, helping to fill the background. A row or two of Oriental Soumak will beat up into the pile row, firm and support it, and sometimes raise it a bit. A row of chaining or twining is also a good method to use before and/or after a pile row. These weaves can be a part of the total design, and colors can add to the over-all effect of different levels on the surface. When Greek Soumak or Oriental Soumak is the slightly raised surface being featured, rows of fine yarn in plain, twill, or basket weave will slip under the Soumak rows and make them more prominent. At the same time, the weaving will become very firm. This is a good method for weaving a rug that is more interesting than a flat weave, but not a truly deep pile.

Add all these surface-interest techniques to your repertory and use them in imaginative ways to bring new dimensions to your textiles.

Looms

The loom used should be suitable for the project. For a very heavy rug, a strong floor-loom is indicated, two or four harnesses, with a good beater. For a rug made up of small units, (see figures 2-6,-7) a frame loom will work. When the technique requires a good bit of plain or pattern weave as a background, a loom with multiple heddles and a beater will be needed. It is feasible to weave a pile fabric on anything from a two-warp box or cardboard loom through vertical or horizontal rug frame-looms, to floor or table looms. Pile-weave pillows are easily made on frame looms of the desired size, and can be woven on around the frame so you are making the back and front in one piece. (See pillows figures 1-8, 2-4.)

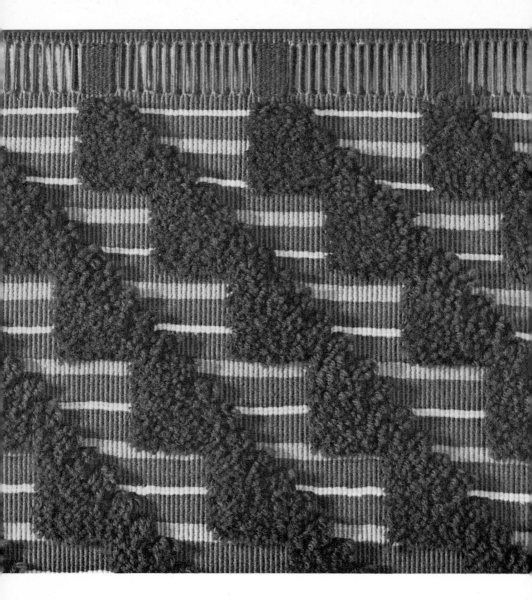

1-10. Ghiordes Knot, cut, in combination with Single Soumak tapestry technique. Note the border of wrapped warps. The pattern was taken from a Northwest Indian basket by weaver Gladys McIlveen.

The plan

When you have decided what to weave, then have selected the proper loom, go on to make your plan or design. Just as in tapestry, if you want a carefully-proportioned pattern, make a cartoon or sketch to follow. One way to plan balanced color and pleasing combinations is to group skeins, balls, or small wads of yarn into an arrangement. Approximate the areas of your design. Move, re-combine, mix, change color proportions and placement, loosely interlace the yarns. Areas of high and low textures can be arranged. You will have a loose simulation of your weaving and a kind of preview of the finished work. This method of color planning is helpful in tapestry weaving, too.

Choose the technique

With the many types of pile weaves possible, take time to select a method that does the best for your project. If you want a sparse, random weave with lots of ground showing, perhaps you will choose the Egyptian Cut Pile or the Highland Guatemalan. For a solid, standing surface, cut or loops, you may use the Ghiordes Knot or Chivas. Study our photographs for effects achieved by the different ways.

Combining methods

A mix of cut, uncut, laid-in, and picked-up pile is easily incorporated in a single weaving. More than one method is interesting to weave as well as to look at. Combine low loops with tall or combed smooth cut pile, in areas or rows. Outline a close-clipped design unit with loops.

Pattern threadings

A ground weave in a woven pattern in two contrasting colors is an effective foil for some areas of raised surface. The pattern can be treadled, and cut pile or loops woven, to accent all or part of it. Or the ground around pattern units can be made in a higher texture, the patterns flat-woven. The endless possible combinations of high and low in two or more colors and yarn sizes give great latitude in achieving a distinctive weaving, obviously hand-woven and different from any other. A single row of low loops effectively outlines a pattern unit or emphasizes lines of the design.

Color choices

You can do anything your designing heart desires in color — where you want it and in what combinations you wish. Strands of yarn for cut pile or weft for picked-up loops can be mixed, or matched.

The most subtle effects are achieved with blending of colors, shades, and yarn sizes. Each tuft or loop can be different from the following one. Color-change, multi-colored wefts, patterns, spots and stripes are so easy to accomplish in pile weaves. The cut-end methods allow different colors in each knot. Where loops are picked up from wefts woven in, several colors can be carried along and any color desired picked up at any place along the row.

1-11. A flat loom-woven pattern enriched by loops.

Change as frequently as your design requires. One favorite way of weaving a cut pile with much blending and mixing is to include one or two basic colors in each pile unit. This gives a common denominator of color throughout, and the whole weaving will look unified. But if you add several different colors to the basic ones, in varying amounts, the surprise differences will make it sparkle. If your careful plans for color don't seem quite right in some places, pile-weft ends can be added or removed — even when the weaving is off the loom. Cut ends can be eased out with a blunt needle. Yarn threaded in a tapestry needle can be added in cut lengths or in loops to add density, or change in shading. Study our examples on page 5.

Warp color and end finishes

The warp color is important if it will be a visible part of the ground weave, selvedge, or a fringed end. More about warps and wefts follows. More about selvedges and end finishes will be found in Part II, Techniques, pages 90-92.

The weaving

Warp

Yarn

A smooth strong yarn, tightly spun, is the best choice. Pulling wefts down over and manipulating the warps to place the pile wefts will tend to fuzz up a yarn that is loosely spun or hairy. Linen, cotton, or wool may be used. Linen or seine twine are good choices for a rug or heavy wall-hanging. Wool should be a tight warp spin, particularly in a rug. Wool worsted works for small pillows and such. Just remember that the wear the weaving will receive is an important factor, as well as the heaviness and density of the pile.

Color

The warp color is important if you plan an integral warp fringe. If you are weaving with a very dark color and want complete coverage, we suggest using a dark warp. It takes a lot of packing-in to cover a white warp with a dark color, especially if the surface is a combined flat and pile weave. With a dark warp, those disconcerting dots of light color won't appear when the weaving is shifted by stepping on, leaning on, or wearing. Of course, should you change plans midway, you can add a different color fringe, or even dye the warp ends if necessary.

Number per inch

This varies with what you are weaving, and all the usual factors of wear, technique, yarn sizes, and so on should be considered. You may need only four to six warp ends for a coarse knotted rug, or on up to fifteen or more for a finer weave. Also consider whether two warp ends will be used as one. Many of the pile methods use warps in pairs. For density, sometimes pile is over-lapped on pairs in succeeding rows. That is, warps number 1 and number 2 are woven as a single warp in the first row, in the second row warps 2 and 3 are woven, then in the third row repeat the first row placement. In pile and tapestry weaves I almost always use double warps. You then have comfortable options — single warps can be woven for close wefts or smaller pattern changes; pairs can be separated to expand or space out the weaving. Be sure that the space between warps will accommodate the knot, wrap, or number of weft yarns without crowding and bunching.

Background

Threading the warp for the ground weave: A plain weave — twill threading — 1, 2, 3, 4, is a most satisfactory one and the usual ground-weave backing a pile surface. Basket weave and diagonal twill are traditional grounds for the Egyptian Cut Pile and the Icelandic Pile, respectively. But do not restrict yourself to these. A pattern weave will add an extra design element, so explore the pattern possibilities, too. The main consideration is that your ground-weave supports and provides a solid enough background for the added wefts. Any of the pile weave methods can be designed to enhance a flat background weave. An area of raised surface will bring importance to an over-all pattern weave with some of the pattern elevated into loops, or cut pile inserted as outline or accent.

• Warp tension. Tension should be taut enough to allow wefts to slide down into place in the wrapping or knotting without stretching the warp, relaxed enough so the wefts can be easily put around the warp, can be lifted or pushed aside when necessary, and allow the laid-in or wrapped wefts to move in close to the preceding row of ground weave.

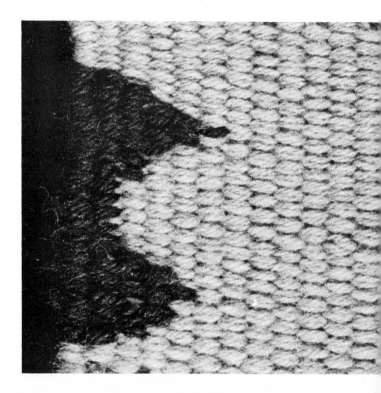

1-12. Extra selvedge wefts as border pattern.

The Selvedge

It is usually a good idea to double one, two, or more of the warps at each selvedge. In rug weaving this is especially important to help give a strong edge and to support the solid ground-weave of the selvedge. Generally rows of pile knots or laid-in pile are not brought out to the very edge, which leaves space that is flat woven. Because of the thickness of the pile areas, these outside rows do not beat in tightly and are loose and uneven.

• Building up the selvedge. To compensate for the heavy pile rows or areas as the weaving progresses, weave in extra, short rows of the ground weft as filler when necessary. Weave in and out over several warps as many times as needed to even up the rows of flat weave and make a strong edge. This is essential in a rug. If your pile surfaces are at a distance from the selvedge these extra rows can become a part of the pattern, by using a contrasting yarn or weaving them in triangles or other shapes, in a utilitarian or a decorative way.

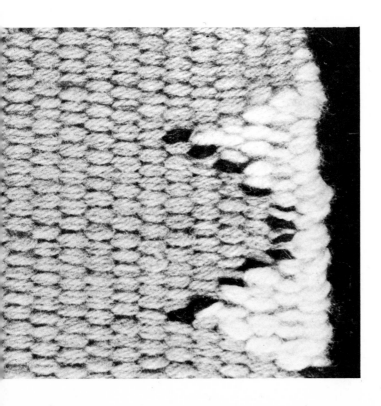

Weft
The pile weft
The sky is the limit in color, yarns, sizes, and spins. The only deciding factor is your imagination, ability, and the project. There is a pile technique that will fit almost any fiber—even stiff, wiry ones. Just don't expect a stiff, slick plastic or a tightly-spun harsh cowhair yarn to make a luxurious, relaxed pile surface! Using many strands as one weft is desirable, especially in pile rug weaving. This not only fills the ground well and makes a rich dense surface, but allows unlimited color combinations and subtle shadings. Use a handful at a time—or a single yarn. Use a continuous weft from a shuttle, or use pre-cut lengths.

The ground weft
Often you may want to use the same yarn as in the warp. This weaves inconspicuous selvedges and headings. The ground weft, to pack in successfully, should be a fairly soft spin. It could match the warp, but be a softer spin and different size. The ground and the pile weft are sometimes the same—in a picked-up loop pattern can be one and the same, with loops picked up then woven flat. The picks between the loops will match, giving a pleasant look of high and low texture.

Warp and weft should work well together for the result you want. If the ground-weave does not blend into the warp and pile rows your fabric will not be tight and firm, but flexible and limp. For example, a hard-twist smooth linen ground weft will not beat in as well as a softer cotton or wool. As in all weaving, put the relaxed weft in on a slight slant so it will not draw in at the selvedge when beaten.

Wefts can be woven in with a shuttle, butterflies, hand-hanks, cut ends, or whatever suits the method you are using. A gauge may be used to insure evenness of pile or loops. A piece of dowel, a pencil, a long knitting needle, strips of heavy cardboard, rulers, fine wire—the gauge can be anything suitable for the depth you want. For making a Rya or Flossa rug, there is a metal gauge made with a groove, and a knife to cut the pile. Cutting can be done in each row, with scissors, as you weave. Cut, remove the gauge, then go on to the next row. Or all cutting can be done after the piece is off the loom. Further shaping, trimming, carving into patterns can be done on the loom while in tension, or later. On a rug, it is sometimes a good idea to do all the cutting of loops after it is finished and placed flat on the floor. You may see a different way than planned—perhaps some areas left uncut, some in different lengths.

The casual effect of a pile that is not precisely trimmed is often the charm of these weaves. Slightly uneven loops, brought up from the background with only the fingers as a gauge, are often more handsome than strictly gauged rows. This is a matter of personal preference, suitability to the weaving, and the design.

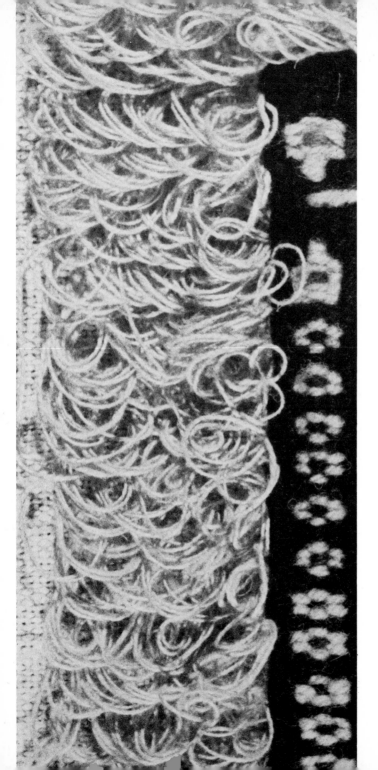

Carving

A very, very dense pile can be carved and shaped in some areas or left shaggy in others. For an elegant, luxurious carved or modeled surface, your pile weave must be extremely compact, with wefts packed in so tightly that they support each other. Allow for tall wefts so the contours can be gradually sloped. Even the shortest pile must be adequate to stay in place. Use a closely-set warp, good wool yarn, and sharp scissors. (Figures 1-2, 1-14, and color page 16.)

Trying out yarns and methods

My epitaph must surely read: "She wove samples!" It is so very important. There is even more reason to sample before starting a pile-weave project than for other kinds of weaving — especially when weaving a rug. You are making something that will take many hours to finish. You are using good, expensive yarns. If the weave is new to you, you must know how to estimate the amount of yarn you will need and just how it fits into the sett of the warp. You will want to do some experiments with color combinations and exact methods, lengths of pile, and density. Do make some samples! It is not a waste of time. Add to your reference file.

How much yarn?

The warp length is figured just about as you figure it for any kind of weaving. Allow for the tie-up at each end of the loom, or for taking the warp around a frame. Add some for headings, hem, and/or warp protection techniques or a warp fringe. Then add a few more inches per yard for take-up in the warp length in the weaving or knotting. If your technique requires using pairs of warp, be certain that the total per inch is an even number. At the beginning or the end of the warp add still more for sampling and experiment.

Estimating the weft. About the best way I know of to do this is to make a sample of the exact method you plan on with the yarns you plan to use. Measure the lengths before you start, and note how many inches of weaving are finished with the measured yarn. Allow a generous amount, because there is always some used to even up the ends, or perhaps there is a slight variation in the tightening of knots, or turnings at the selvedge, which will take up more. If you have a limited amount of yarn in one color and want it scattered throughout, divide it into bunches and use just that amount in a given area. Using pre-cut ends, you can toss all the colors together as you would ingredients for a salad; then pick them up in bundles, as they come. Surprisingly, the distribution of color will be fairly regular.

1-14. Detail of the elegant carved pile by Fritzi Oxley shown in color on page 16. (Photograph by Beverly Rush.)

And now—

Having suggested, listed, detailed, and warned about what to do and what not to do when weaving a pile surface, we come to Part II, the Pile-Weave Techniques and how to do them. Descriptions and directions with drawings of procedures and photographs of examples follow.

2-1. A composition-sampler of pile weaves, with dovetail tapestry joining the blocks of color. Across the bottom, Ghiordes Knot loops. Left column, from bottom: Icelandic, Ghiordes Double Loops, Chivas, Single-warp Spanish, and Ancient, Sehna, right and left. Chaining, Soumak and slits across the top. Right column, from bottom: Ghiordes Knot loops, Czech Cut Pile Shag, Granitos, Slip Loop, Ghiordes Knot and Lark's Head (Cow Hitch) in all directions.

Part II
Pile Weave Techniques and
how to do them

As you practice these techniques we suggest that you refer to the general instructions in Part I from time to time.

Variations

Every time you try new methods of knotting or looping for a pile surface remember to pull ends, raise loops, and see in what other ways you can make a secure pile from the basic type. Collingwood's **Rug Weaving** is a prime source for different ways to use Soumaks and other knots for raised surfaces. Loops can be pulled out from the standard Oriental Soumak—Ghiordes Knot ends can be pulled out in loops—Greek Soumak can be the basis of a knobby pile, and so on. These variations are included in the directions that follow. (Figure 2-1, and C-4 on color page 21.)

1 Ghiordes Knot (Turkish, Rya, Flossa, Two-warp Oriental) (D-1 — D-5)

This is probably the most satisfactory and most-used rug knot the world around. While it is known under different names, and identified with specific weaving styles, the basic technique is the same: wefts put over and around warp pairs, using cut wefts or continuous weft over a gauge, which is then cut or left in loops. The working drawings D-1—D-5 show where the yarn goes. The photographs of examples give you an idea of how the different uses of the knot look. (Figures 2-1—2-7.)

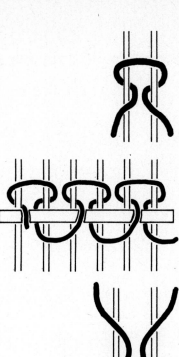

D-1. Ghiordes Knot, pre-cut weft.

D-2. Ghiordes Knot, over gauge.

D-3. Ghiordes Knot, upside down.

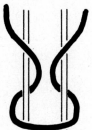

D-4. Lark's Head (Cow Hitch). Pile slants sideways, over one warp.

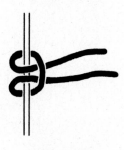

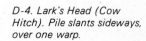

D-5. Ghiordes Knot, double loops.

C-5. **Blue-eyed Spring.** *Pile weave woven in a circle. Warps are held by the hoop-loom, and warp ends and wefts are plaited and knotted.*

C-6. *An arrangement of pile weaves, with tapestry dove-tail joining of the color-blocks.*

C-7. *High and low textures, loops, cut ends, and the Soumaks.*

C-8. *Wool rug, Ghiordes Knot, in the process of being woven on a vertical rug loom. Clipped ends are closely packed, and the design and texture has qualities of an Oriental rug. Weaver, Mildred Sherwood (Photograph by Mildred Sherwood.)*

Ghiordes Knot every which way—cut ends or loops

The faithful Ghiordes Knot is an accommodating one. You can weave it in upside down and sideways, as well as the conventional method with pile slanting down or standing.

Upside down: Pull ends or loops through above the weft that goes across the top of the warp. This takes the pile away from the weaver, instead of bringing it down. With some rows up and some rows down, you can surround areas of ground weave with a hedge of pile weave. (Figures 2-4, 2-5, 2-14, and D-3.)

Sideways: Put cut pile weft over a warp in a Lark's Head hitch (Cow Hitch), with cut ends coming out to the right or to the left. This is the same way Macramé cords are mounted, or the warp on a bag loom. Cut your pile wefts a bit more than twice the length you want the finished pile length. Fold over so ends are even. Put the loop under the warp and pull ends through loop, securing it to the warp by pulling up snug. If you want the ends to the left of the warp, put the loop under to the left. Pull ends through to the left. Reverse for a right-facing pile—loop under to right, pull ends through to the right. (See D-4.)

Smooth the pile down for the greatest effect of horizontal direction. Leave enough ground weave and space to show the complete knot and the special effect of this variation as a design element.

2-2. Detail of Ghiordes Knot worked over a gauge: uncut at the right, cut at the left. Handspun wool. (Photograph by William Eng.)

2-3. Miniature loops for a
flat rug with many changes
of color. Woven of very fine
wools on a linen warp.
Shown slightly larger than
the actual weaving. Pile
weave does not have to be
tall and dense.

Ghiordes-Knot Double Loops

A variation where loops instead of cut ends are pulled through. This way of making the comfortable Ghiordes Knot is great fun to do, goes quickly, and the effect is very perky. It gives a good full pile coverage. The pile weft is put around and up between the two warps as usual, but this time you bend the cut ends, grasping the double yarn and pulling it out as a loop rather than a single end. This is done with each end coming up between the warps, so you have two loops and two cut ends. If you use two wefts as one you will have double-double loops, and four cut ends in each unit, which fills the surface very thickly with the raised pile (D-5). The cut ends can be tucked under, but they add to the full texture giving a pleasing effect with both loops and cut ends. Our example in figure 2-8 was done with single, very large rug wool. One warp was left between the loop-knots. It is possible to do this with a continuous weft, but a bit awkward and slow as the right end is cut after each loop is made. We found it best to use pre-cut wefts.

2-4. The pile weave pillow is Ghiordes Knot in two directions, on a basket-weave ground. The tapestry weave pillow has a joining along the top, which makes a fringe — the warp ends are knotted and chained together. Courtesy Nancy Davidson and Mr. and Mrs. Geoffrey Tennant.

One way to do it: Using both hands, put the cut weft over, around, and up between two warps as in a regular Ghiordes Knot. Then push ends up, forming loops. Hold the left cut end while pulling the loops through and tightening around the warps. Slip your finger tip through each loop as a gauge, and tug to tighten. Do a sample to measure the amount of yarn in your height and set. Our example took about eight inches of weft to make loops and ends approximately one inch long, in heavy rug wool set at about five warps per inch.

Weaving a rug in units to be joined

For an area rug, units are designed and woven to be joined in a number of different ways. This design idea is based on Roman Numerals—one on each square unit. The squares will be sewn together firmly, but they can be taken apart and rearranged to make a rug of a different shape, or just to turn the individual patterns around. The two units shown are the I and II (figures 2-6, 2-7). The Vs and Xs add more variety, and make many interesting changes of the over-all pattern. To try out the flexible patterns, we drew the numbers on small squares of paper, and played with combinations—it seemed like an idea with lots of potential. For a unifying line throughout, a band is woven at top and bottom on each unit. Part of the whole concept of module squares was for a new household. With additional furniture, many moves to other rooms, a rug of different proportions might be needed. The units can be put together as a long runner, two-units wide, a square rug several units across, an L-shape, or what you will.

The method

The pile weave is Ghiordes Knot worked over a gauge and cut. All wool. (See figure 1-7.) The color is a blend of deep gold tones, with the numerals and bands in a blend of golden browns and the same gold-tone yarn. The pile weft is made up of five strands of yarn in three sizes and colors. Several rows of plain weave are between the knot rows. The ground weft is dark brown wool, hidden by the close rows of pile. Knots are worked to the outside double warp, making a firm selvedge for the joining. But since the pile covers the joining the effect is of a rug woven all in one piece. On the warp ends, a narrow hem will be turned and the pile will also cover the joinings there.

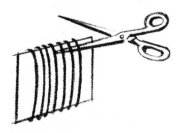

2-5. Ghiordes Knot all ways, with a strip of Iceland sheepskin. Shown in color on page 21.

D-6. One way to cut multiple weft ends for cut pile. Wind yarn around a cardboard. Cut. Do not wind too tightly — the cut strands will be too short if you stretch yarn when winding.

2-6, -7. Two units of the Roman Numeral rug, designed to be joined in changeable combinations. 2-6) Roman numeral *II* section in progress on a frame loom.
2-7) Roman numeral *I* section just as it was cut from the loom.

2 Slip Loop (D-7)

Pile weft is wrapped around one warp and brought out in a loop. A solid line of weft runs along the top of a row of loops when they are made one after the other with no warps skipped in between. This effect is so orderly and neat that it creates a good design element when rows are spaced with ground weave between to show this feature. A small example of slip loops is shown in figure 2-8. The loops can be flat and regular, or small and grouped, or bunched-in for a dense pile. Try them going in two directions. Unless they are tightly beaten in, one hard tug and the loops will pull out. In a clinging wool yarn they can be tightened around the warp to stay in place very well.

D-7. Slip Loop.

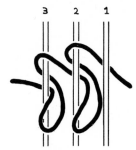

How to do it

Work with a long weft in hand-hank for the best result. From right to left: Weave under warp 1 of the loop unit, tucking the end in around the outside warp at the selvedge. Then over warp 2. With left fingers, push the weft down under warp 2, and to the right. With right fingers, grasp the doubled weft and pull up in a loop between warps 1 and 2. Tighten in place around the warp by pulling the top or right side of the loop. Adjust the length by a pull on the left or free end of the weft. For a continuous row of loops, continue on over warp 3, loop out between warps 3 and 2, and so on. If a space is wanted between loops, weave over and under a few warps before starting another wrap and loop.

2-8. A sampler to show several loop techniques. From bottom: Chivas, Ghiordes Knot Double Loops, Granitos, Slip Loop, Ghiordes Knot loops upside down. Greek Soumak and rows of plain weave.

3 Sehna (Persian) Rug Knot (D-8A, B)

This very old traditional method of making pile rugs is a satisfactory one for many reasons. The surface is well covered, because the ends of the pile weft emerge from every warp space and many knots per inch can be put in close together. It is quite economical of yarn, since most of it is on the surface. The wrapping is around just one warp. The unit consists of a wrap around one warp with ends above and below the next warp. It is usually worked with pre-cut lengths. It can be woven with a continuous weft, leaving a loop on the surface before continuing to the next wrapped unit. There seems to be a difference of opinion and interpretation of the terms "Right-hand" and "Left-hand" Sehna. The difference is in the name, not the method. One is based on the structure — the other is based on the appearance. Our preference, based on a study of the structure, seems logical thus: Call it Left-hand when the weft is wrapped on the left warp of the pair (even though the ends slant to the right). Call it Right-hand when the weft is wrapped around the right-hand warp of the pair (with ends slanting to the left).

Work either or both ways in one weaving. The pile is directional, with ends slanting to right or left. A windblown pile is made by working the left- and right-hand wraps in alternate rows, or changing every few warps. (See figure 2-1, and C-6 on color page 40.)

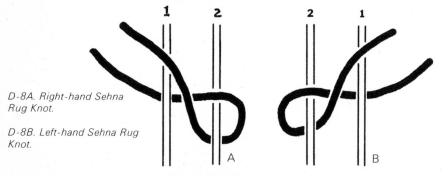

D-8A. Right-hand Sehna Rug Knot.

D-8B. Left-hand Sehna Rug Knot.

How to Do It

Right-hand Sehna Cut Pile: Work from left, with a pre-cut end. Leave end out, weave under warp 1, over warp 2, around and under, up and out. Skip one warp, then repeat for the next unit. The wrap is on the right warp of the pair, the ends slant to the left.

Left-hand Sehna Cut Pile: Work from the right. Leave end out, weave under warp 1, over 2, around and under, up and out. Skip one warp before beginning the next unit. The warp is on the left warp of the pair, the ends slant to the right.

Always weave at least two rows of tabby before and after each pile row, beating in very firmly. This will hold the pile in place, and rows can be very tightly packed or spaced with wide rows of firm tabby. The pile will hold. With this method, you can insert the ends in areas or spots, picking out isolated patterns. Until you learn the sequence, it helps to chant as you go: "Under, over, around and under, up and out!"

4 Single-warp Spanish Knot (D-9A, B)

This is a wrapped, cut pile. Economical of yarn since it goes around only one warp, it can be made with only an inch of weft. It depends upon the ground weave to keep it in place. It works up quickly, once you get the system going, and have pre-cut wefts. It can be done with continuous weft, but this is slow because you must stop and cut after each wrap. (Figure 2-9, also see C-6 on color page 40.)

2-9. Single-warp Spanish Knot done in a fuzzy acrylic rug yarn and worsted weight, with ground in stripes from alternate rows of two weft colors.

D-9A. Single-warp Spanish Knot.

D-9B. System of placing knots on alternate warps in rows.

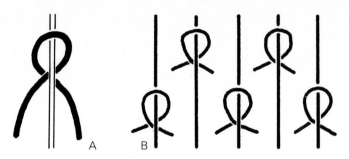

How to do it

Traditionally, one warp is skipped between each knot, then, in the next row, the wefts are put around the warps that were skipped in the first row, thus a full pile is made with no striped effect.

Place weft over warp and, with both hands, take ends down, cross and bring out on top between adjacent warps. (See D-9A, figure 2-1, and C-6 on color page 40.) It is only as secure as your woven rows before and after, so use a ground weft that will close in, and beat very firmly. Wool will make the most satisfactory fabric in this technique. The Spanish Cut Pile on a single warp is similar to the Ancient Cut Pile, which follows.

5 Ancient Cut Pile (Old French) (D-10)

This method is about as fast to do as the One-warp Spanish Cut Pile. A little more secure than the Spanish, and the ends lie down flat. The Spanish cut ends kick up in work, and only lie flat after the binding row of weft is put in. (Figure 2-1.)

D-10. Ancient — on one warp.

How to do it

Work from left to right with pre-cut wefts. Put the weft under one warp, double into a loop at the right side of the warp, with cut end passing under the warp to the left. Bring left end over warp and down through loop. Slide gently down in place while pulling on each end to tighten around warp and even the ends. Close rows of tabby are necessary before and after the pile rows.

6 Icelandic Cut Pile (D-11)

This technique was used in the fashioning of a cloak in Iceland hundreds of years ago. On a diagonal twill background, shaggy tags of wool were inserted, providing a long pile. Partly laid-in and partly wrapped, the method results in a surface that can be well covered, or a pile that shows some of the background. An example is shown in the lower left corner of figure 2-1 and center bottom of C-1, color page 5.

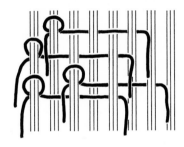

D-11. Icelandic Cut Pile.

How to do it

Tie up: Twill, 1, 2, 3, 4. Treadled as a diagonal twill, 1, 2; 2, 3; 3, 4; 4, 1.

For the pile weave, use pre-cut wefts or weft in a small hand-hank.

The sequence, in rows:

Several rows of twill weave as a heading.

Alternate rows of pile weave are staggered, so the pile will be evenly distributed, but not in fixed vertical rows.

Use the warp in pairs. Pile-row number one begins on the first warp pair. Pile-row number two begins on the second warp pair. Pile-row number three begins on the first warp pair, and so on. Several rows of twill weave are woven and firmly beaten between the rows of pile.

One unit of the pile weave:

From left, take weft under warp pairs, up, over, and around, then weave over and under four warp pairs, to the right. The left and right ends will be on the surface, and should be about one inch long. Skip three warp pairs before putting in the next pile unit. Continue across the row.

This is the Icelandic cloak system, but the separate pile wefts can be placed in any formation — rows, staggered, or hit and miss, for whatever pile effect you wish. Because one end of the weft is well anchored by wrapping, the wefts will not easily pull out.

Double-face Pile

A two-sided pile is a challenge, but worth the extra time. It is an appropriate fabric for a cape or jacket, a coverlet or throw, a room divider or space hanging. Having tried this weave on both a floor loom and a frame loom, we found the frame loom easier by

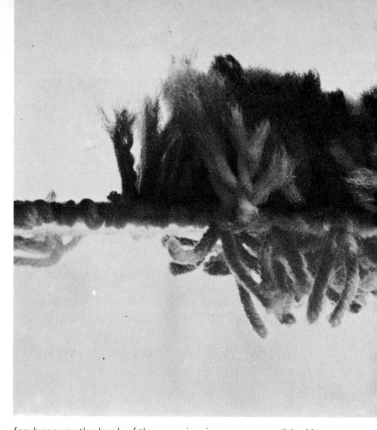

far, because the back of the weaving is more accessible. However, with a bit of practice, you will find it is not too difficult to weave two sides at a time. Our sampling for a double-pile crib cover was woven on a four-harness floor loom. The pile method is the Icelandic Cut Pile, which worked well for this purpose. Made of acrylic yarn for washability. The warp and ground are light yellow worsted, sleyed double in a 12 dent reed, 6 per inch. The ground weft is double, wound on a shuttle. The weft on the top surface is pale blue rug yarn. The pile on the other side is a clear red-orange worsted. Pile wefts used are from small hand-hanks. (Figures 2-10, -11, -12.)

The procedure

Four rows of twill, yellow worsted.

From left, blue pile weft in small hand bobbin. Over one warp pair (see D-11) and to the right, under and over four warp pairs. The end is brought out and cut to one inch in length. Skip three warp pairs and repeat across the width.

Weave four rows of twill, yellow.

Begin a row of orange pile, putting in the same as above, but push the cut ends down through to the under side. Repeat across the width.

Weave one row of yellow, then put in a row of blue pile for the

top surface. Repeat, putting three or four rows of twill weave between the pile rows, and just one row between the upper and lower rows of pile. With this sequence, you will have a pile that is airy and soft, but some of the ground weave shows, with dots of the red-orange showing against the yellow as background for the blue pile. On the reverse side, dots of blue show in the background under the red-orange pile. This is just one variation of the idea. The pile sides can be quite dense or one long, one short; one dense, the other side very scattered. For a cape or coat, the inside could be short and sheared — the top side could be longer, or closely cut with shaggy borders. A room divider can have quite different effects on each side — the weaves will all look related because of the common ground weave. Try some double-pile weaves — you will feel quite accomplished! Other laid-in techniques can be used as well as the Icelandic method. Also some woven overshot patterns clipped on both sides. We tried that for a coverlet, because it is a good holding pile.

When the pile is put in on an open shed, it goes quickly, because the pairs of warp that are up are automatically selected and ready to be wrapped.

Double-face pile is not a new idea — weavings using this double surface have been found in ancient Egypt and elsewhere.

2-11

2-12

7 Egyptian Cut Pile (D-12)

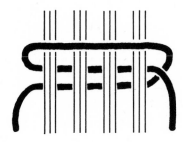

D-12. Egyptian Cut Pile.

Early examples of this technique were woven in slub linen, with the shaggy pile smoothed down. The background was completely covered. Although the traditional ground was basket weave (figure 2-13) it can be done on any kind of plain or pattern weave. Our big floor pillow, figure 2-14, was done in random Oriental Soumak weave of unspun wool. The groups of Egyptian Cut Pile ends — handspun wool — are laid in over different numbers of warp for wide and narrow accents. Because the weft wraps around and three passes of weft are in each unit, the fabric is given added strength and thickness. The One-warp Ancient Cut Pile is similar to this Egyptian pile. The wrap is essentially the same, but the Egyptian extends over several warps.

When a loom with a shed is used, work on an open shed. Treadle so the warps you are covering are UP. This speeds the process quite a bit because the warps are already selected and ready. When the pile weft is put around every warp in a row, work all the way across on the up position, then change shed, weave the background, and continue with pile rows or areas. The pile rows can be staggered, or each unit can be made on the same group of warps over all. One or more wefts can be used as your design requires — for a thick or a flat surface.

Many uses are found for this neat, secure way of putting in a cut pile. A good one to use when making a two-sided pile fabric (see Icelandic). High and low, long and short can be combined in one piece. The pile can be dense, sparse, or spaced. Fine for borders and trims, and isolated spots or rows. The cut ends are bridged with an overshot and a continuous line on the surface shows when ends are close, beginning and ending between the same two warps. The spacing on the big cloud pillow (2-14) is very random — the spacing on the example in figure 2-13 is regular, with four wefts used as one, over four pairs of warp, skipping one pair in between. Worked over the same warps in each succeeding row, with pile length approximately even throughout.

2-13. Example of Egyptian
Cut Pile on basket-weave
ground.

Right. 2-14. **Clouds at Twenty-thousand-feet** *(top).*
*Egyptian Cut Pile in sky blue,
on a big floor pillow of white
unspun wool, Oriental
Soumak weave. The dark
pillow at bottom is wool,
Ghiordes Knot in two
directions, with wrapped
tassels for trim.*

How to do it

Work with cut pieces of weft, or from a hand bobbin, cutting the
end at the right after each wrapping.

Working from left to right: Left cut end hangs, the longest end
at the right is the working end. Carry this under several warps,
back over the same warps, then under again to the right, with the
end brought out to the surface. D-12 on preceding page shows
how the right weft-end emerges. This sequence locks the right-
hand ends in so they lie flat like the left ones. For a close pile,
begin the next unit between the same two warps, where the
previous end came out. Or warps can be skipped between the
extra wefts. Rows of basket weave are woven between the rows
of pile. We prefer to work with pre-cut ends, cutting a number of
them at once. (See D-6, one way to cut wefts.)

As with all pile weaves, work a few, then measure the amount of
yarn used, as there is no real rule for just how much is required
for a given plan.

8 Granitos (Spanish Confite)(D-13)

A low looped surface comes to us from Spain, via bedspreads woven by Spanish brides for their dowry chests. Patterns of flowers, names, and dates were woven in this loop technique. This is a wrapped weave, with weft winding back and forth over the warps. It is a secure one that will not pull out. In structure it seems to be related to the open-work Spanish Lace because, before they are pushed down into place, the loops spiral up in the same fashion. One loop unit consists of weft woven in, then wrapped over two warps, stepped over one warp and wrapped over two again. When slid down into place against the previous woven row, two flat loops are on top. The size of the loop varies according to the number of warps it covers, whether a single weft is used, or a number of wefts used as one. The loops can be pulled down almost flat or left a bit looser for a higher texture. Rows of tabby are woven between the loop rows. Color is easily introduced in rows or spots. (See figure 2-8.)

Granitos is an apt name, as the texture is a coarse, grainy one. A very useful technique, this, for everything from rugs to clothing and household textiles. When the loops are low and narrow, it would be satisfactory in upholstery fabric.

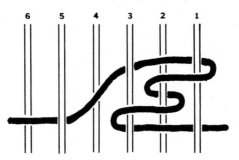

D-13. Granitos (Spanish Confite).

How to do it

The working drawing D-13 shows clearly the path of the yarn over the numbered warps, working from right to left. It can be woven from left to right also. When all passes have been made, push down with fingers or beater to the row of tabby ground weave, which is woven both before and after the units of loops. Several rows of ground are woven between loop rows. A small shuttle, or a small flat ball of weft is easiest for making the loops, with the ground-weave yarn woven in with a regular shuttle.

9 Highland Guatemalan Cut Pile (D-14A, B)

This one is perfect for areas of flat weave plus some cut pile. You can put the pattern just where you wish. The classic method results in vertical bands of cut ends, with the ground showing between (figure 2-15). A very good method to use in rugs, borders, or spot textures on draperies — on a skirt or poncho, on pillows.

A   B

D-14A, B. Two ways to place cut ends in Highland Guatemalan Cut Pile.

Below. 2-15. Highland Guatemalan Cut Pile in stripes of orange, brown, yellow on a brown wool plain weave. Courtesy Gary and Sheri Wilson.

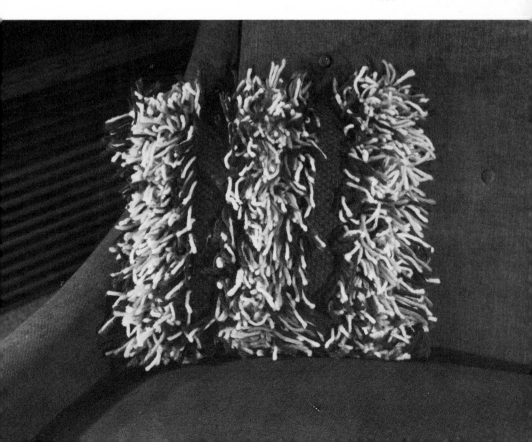

How to do it

For regular vertical stripes of pile: Plain weave ground. A loom with two or four harnesses is adequate and the best choice, since the ground weave is woven from a shuttle. For small units, like a pillow, however, it can be done on a frame loom, with or without a shedding device. Our small pillow, figure 2-15, was done on a frame loom. Cut lengths are laid in under four or five warps. (See drawing D-14.) The next weft is laid in with ends emerging from between the same warps as the previous weft. Continue across the row, placing ends under each succeeding group of warps. Treadle so these warps are up and the shed is open to put in the pile wefts. Then weave rows of plain weave between, as many as you need. Now that you know the classic method, you can do any number of variations. Space ends unevenly, at random, or in a geometric block or stripe pattern. Vary the lengths of pile in one design, or have each end a different length. Use multiple wefts as one. Weave a patterned background, or add color in the warp. Use different yarn sizes. Combine with needle-made stitches on some of the ground weave, or pull up some loops.

The usual pile weave suggestions also apply here: Weave some units of laid-in pile to give you an estimate of the amount of yarn you will need and the length of pile best for your plan; beat the rows of ground weave firmly.

10 Czech Cut Pile (D-15A, B)

A random, nicely tousled-looking cut pile is found in shepherd's cloaks in Czechoslovakia — no doubt inspired by the coats of the sheep. Cut ends are put into the warp and the ends come from between different pairs of warps so the effect is non-directional — the cut ends lie in different directions and at different angles. Done on a plain weave ground, with tabby rows between. The units of three wefts can be staggered or put in at random, as dense a pile as required. One version shows wrapping at one point — the other is all laid-in.

D-15. Czech Cut Pile Shag.
A. Laid in, one warp wrapped.
B. Laid in, with no wrapping.

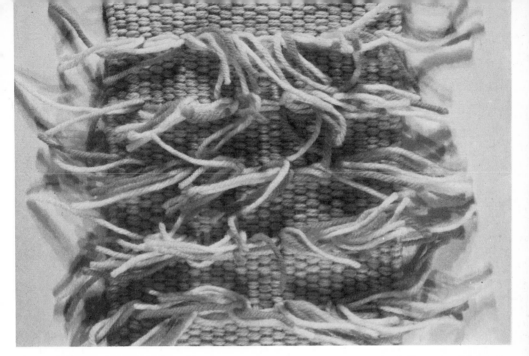

How to Do it

With three wefts put in before any ground weave is woven, you will find it very important to build up the selvedge with extra short rows of ground weft as you go along. (See pages 31-2.) Work with cut ends or continuous warp from a shuttle. A loom with a shedding device and beater is the best choice, but weaving can be done on a frame or other simple loom.

Three weft ends are laid in. Six pile ends are on the surface. Study drawings D-15A, B to follow the yarn paths.

With one wrap (D-15A)

From left to right: Leave left end of weft hanging on surface, then go under three warps and cut the right end to pile length. Under the same first warp, then over and under for seven warps, around the seventh and back over and under four; cut end to pile length. Starting with the same first warp, under, over, under. Cut right end and leave on surface. This is one unit, employing one wrap.

Another way (D-15B)

None of the weft is wrapped around any warp as in D-15A above. In method D-15B all three wefts are woven over and under, emerging at different places, using a total of nine warps. Bring the ends out at warps 3, 5, and 9, for instance.

A very rich pile surface will result when more than one weft is used as one — each of the three insertions can be multiple, and all in different colors for subtle blends. Pile rows can be very closely spaced so ground is completely covered. Very good for a shaggy rug. A wide-spaced pile would make a good inside face for a coat.

2-16. Example of Czech Cut Pile Shag.

11 Picked-up Loops (D16)

The classification of picked-up loops covers an extremely wide span of years and various methods. Loops of weft are raised from the background of the weaving in a number of different ways, with fingers or some kind of tool such as a crochet hook, pointed stick, or knitting needle. They may be put over a gauge, or formed less precisely with the fingers. Loops make the units of pattern in an all-over design, a solid looped surface, or separate rows. Coptic portrait miniatures were woven with loops forming the face and head; loops are found in rugs, bedspreads, on clothing in almost every weaving culture — Peruvian, Mexican, Guatemalan, African, European, Colonial-American, and others.

D-16. Picked-up Loops, over a gauge.

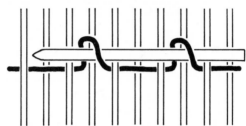

2-17. Picked-up loops with cut ends.

Designing for looped surfaces

The choice of warp and weft yarn is most important, and the two must work well together, in size and spin. Because there is no wrapping or knotting around the warp, the loops depend upon a tight ground weave for security. A picked-up loop method is best to use in a fabric that will not get a lot of abrasive wear or be subject to catching by heels. Exceptions might be where low loops are picked up in fine cotton textiles — like some Mexican ones — where washing will shrink the ground and slightly mat the wefts so they do not pull out as easily. On rugs, a liquid Latex backing will help to hold the loops in place.

Color

Color change is completely flexible and each loop could be a different color by carrying many colors in the weft and picking up the different ones. The simplest color variation is one for the background and one for the loops.

NOTE: That when loops are not brought to the outside selvedges it will be necessary to build up the selvedges with extra, short wefts woven in and out;

That soft yarns, such as wool, will make a better looped textile than smooth, stiff yarns;

That smooth yarns will work if the warp is set quite close and the ground weave yarns are very fine and beaten in;

That, usually, it is not a good idea to clip picked-up loops. For a clipped pile, it is better to choose a technique where some of the weft is wrapped or knotted around the warp;

That loops can be picked up on any kind of a firm ground weave — patterned or plain.

2-18. A baby wrapper from Africa, made of white handspun cotton with a center section of loops, like terry cloth. Ivadan, Nigeria. From **Introducing West African Cloth,** *with permission from the author, Kate P. Kent, and the Denver Museum of Natural History.*

2-19. Unfinished wall
hanging, in an assortment of
pile weaves: Across the
bottom; Massed picked-up
loops. Far left column, from
bottom: Single Picked-up
Loops in chenille, Basket
Weave, Ghiordes Knot cut
and uncut. Near left, from
bottom: Icelandic Cut Pile,
countered Oriental Soumak,
Chivas.

How to do it

D-16, page 64, shows loops picked up on a gauge. Whether loops
are drawn up by gauge, pick, or fingers, the procedure is the same:
A row of weft is woven, and the loops are taken up to the surface.
They may be raised up at every warp, or spaced. Work from right
to left, or left to right, or in both directions in one piece. The
loops will have a slight directional slant, which can be a part of
your design. Be sure to work with the shuttle or "feeder" end of
the yarn ahead of your looping. When you pick up loops in isolated
areas, the ends of weft can be brought around and tucked into the
shed and will hold when the ground weave is woven and beaten
in. Or the loop weft can be carried along with the ground weft
even in areas that will be all flat weave.

One variation of the many that are possible:

Twisted Loops. When each loop is raised, then twisted a half
turn, then beaten in, the loop will be held a little tighter, and has
a slightly different appearance than the regular raised loop. It
tends to lie flat and each loop overlaps the other slightly.

Not to be Overlooked

Following are some of the pile-weave techniques we think are important to include, even though we have space for only a brief introduction to them. Our pages just refuse to stretch for a thorough "how to" on this group but we feel they are too important and interesting to omit. So here they are, with a short description and a drawing or photograph. We urge you to search them out and explore them. (See bibliography.)

12 Tibetan Rug Knot (D-17)

D-17. Tibetan Rug Knot. One unit, over pairs of warp and gauge.

We highly recommend your study of this rug knot and hope our sketch and comments intrigue you. It makes a rich, long-wearing pile, swings along rapidly, is worked over a gauge. Easy color change inspires an all-over pattern.

13 Eigg Cut Pile (D-18)

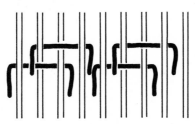

D-18. Eigg Cut Pile.

An early-day technique of weaving a cut pile comes from the Isle of Eigg. Cut ends are laid in with ends out on the surface. When beaten very firmly into rows of ground weave, the ends can be as short as an inch and still be practical. The unit of pile consists of a row of laid-in wefts under and over three warps, tabby rows in between, and the next row laid in, offset by one warp. The resulting fabric is a well-covered surface of short, straight, flat pile. It is similar to the Highland Guatemalan method.

14 Chivas

From Guatemala comes a picked-up loop called *Chivas*. It resembles a close, dense pelt, when in an over-all pile surface. Natural wools in shades of white through gray to black make rich and beautiful rugs with loops picked up in geometric patterns and stripes. (See figures 2-1, 2-8, and C-6 on color page 40.)

How to do it

Two loop wefts are woven in at the same time. Loops are lifted all the way across or in pattern areas. The loops are picked up together, but they separate and make a full, loopy surface with each loop following its own direction. Use a gauge for even loops, or pull them up with the fingers for a more casual surface.

The background weave, because of the double weft, will tend to distort when spots of pattern are put in. But with careful beating and extra ground wefts woven in where necessary there should be no problem in weaving a good textile. On some items, this can be exploited as a part of your design.

The ground weave is usually plain weave, but Chivas can be picked up on any pattern weave.

The loop wefts are taken up along the selvedge until needed again, and can be brought out in small half-circles as they travel in and out of the pattern rows. This strengthens the selvedge as well as enhancing it.

15 Boutonné (D-19A, B)

D-19A. Boutonné, loops picked up from plain-weave ground.

D-19B. Boutonné pattern style. Loops brought up from short rows of pattern weft.

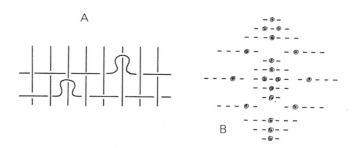

A

B

A French-Canadian version of picked-up loops. Stars and mosaic-like geometric patterns are typical, often appearing in woven rugs and other textiles such as tablecloths. A weft in a color strongly contrasting with the background is woven in, then small loops are raised at intervals. The pattern wefts are laid in to define the shape of the design. (See color page 5.)

16 Oriental Soumak (D-20)

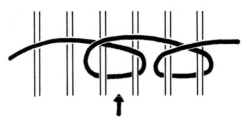

D-20. Oriental Soumak. Arrow shows where loop can be elevated.

A low-profile surface weave that can be counted as a kind of pile weave, and can be made to give a raised loop-like face. The arrow on the drawing D-20 indicates where a loop can be pulled out as the weft is taken over and back around the warps. The method of bringing the loop out is like that of the slip loop. The possibilities in this technique are interesting, as the loops can be raised throughout, or only in some places. When the Soumak is countered — that is, worked in opposite directions in alternate rows, giving an arrow look, even more surface interest occurs. The Soumak rows lend themselves to large scale yarns and multiple wefts to raise them in a ridge. Several rows of fine ground weft will also help elevate the rows. (See figures 2-14, 2-20.)

2-20. Loops combined with Oriental Soumak.

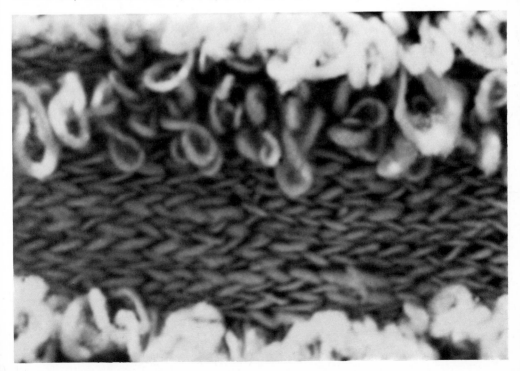

17 Greek Soumak (D-21 and 2-21)

Greek Soumak is a very useful technique to add to your store. It covers a warp quickly and creates a wonderfully knobby surface. Effective in large yarn, multiple wefts used as one, and can be woven in any direction. Putting more than the classic three knots on each warp before moving to the next warp results in a high knotted texture. The top and bottom borders of wall hanging shown on color page 5 were woven with large rug wool. The rows of Greek Soumak alternate direction. Both Oriental and Greek Soumak are in sections of figure 1-8.

D-21. Greek Soumak.

Below. 2-21. Greek Soumak is the technique used in the two pillows at bottom.

How to do it

Follow the arrows and the path of the yarn in drawing D-21. It is not necessary to beat the knots into place, as the pulling down of each knot will settle it in. If you do want a tighter fabric, you can push the rows of knots together with your fingers. It is not necessary to weave rows of ground between rows of Greek Soumak, but for a different effect, it can be done.

18 Chaining (D-22)

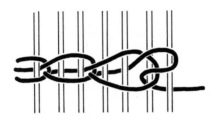

D-22. Chaining.

Chaining, with most of the weft on the top of the fabric, can be considered as a surface interest weave. It is also a good base to hold lengths of wool pile, looped through as you chain or inserted after the chaining is completed. With heavy yarn and several strands, a chain row becomes a rounded ridge. Chain several loops above the warp, then continue around the warps, and you will have a small mound raised higher than the row. This has good possibilities for an accent, or for a high and low rug surface. (See figure 2-1, and C-6 on color page 40.)

How to do it

From left to right:
The weft is laid under all warps, with a loop at the left end, at the outside warp. The weft is picked up from under the warp and brought up in loops between warps. Study drawing D-22 and you will see where the weft yarn comes up into the loop and where it is under the warp. Chaining can be done back and forth, resulting in an arrow or knitted look; or each row can be chained from the same side each time. When the chain row is completed, and not returned, cut the end, pull that end up through the last loop to tighten and lock the loop.

19 Weft Twining as a base for a Pile Weft (D-23)

Peruvian weavers, New Zealand Maoris, and weavers from other cultures found that twining was a perfect base for the insertion of pile wefts — whether they were feathers, tags of wool, bits of cloth, or fibers. The double twist of the twining holds the insertions securely.

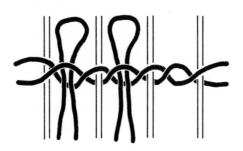

D-23. Weft Twining. Cut wefts inserted.

Loops in Twining

One of the two twining wefts can be pulled up into a loop over every other warp. With rows of twining before and after the twined-loop rows, the loops will be tightly held in.

Another way: Use three twining wefts — one single, one double. Pull one from the double weft down into a loop, making the turn (half or full) with the pair of wefts. Put the looped weft back in with the other and continue twining with two and one wefts until another loop is required by your design. It seems to work well when a loop is pulled out every other twist. Then, for rows of full loop pile, the loops can be pulled out from alternate spaces. This method makes it possible to carry a loop weft in a different color and/or yarn than the ground twining.

Inserting cut ends

A cut end of weft can be put over and under the twining wefts before the turn is made. Either a half or full turn can then be made.

Another way: Double the cut pile weft. Make a half turn, lay the extra weft with loop at top, between the twining wefts. Make another half turn, then continue around the next warp. (See D-23.) The loop at the top can be pulled down into the twining, or pulled up as a part of the design, giving a pattern surface of loops and cut ends. With a twist on each side, the pile weft is held quite securely and twining rows before and after will help to hold.

Feathers, wool strips, yarn, leaves — all can be added in on the rows of twining. Do your experimenting with two or three colors, so you can follow the path of each yarn.

20 Loom-controlled Pile Weaves

Not all pile weaves or raised-surface weavings are done by the hands alone. Many of the loom-threaded pattern weaves with overshots make satisfactory and interesting pile weaves. These are different, and very effective, because parts of the ground-weave pattern are emphasized and picked out in a short cut pile. The major requirement in choosing an overshot weave to clip into a pile is that the extra floating weft is tied into the weave with enough warps, so it will not simply fall out. Weaves for this purpose require a closely sett warp. It is usually best to have a warp that is finer than the weft. This not only produces a firmer ground but it also sets off the pattern woven in a heavier yarn. (Figures 2-22, -23, -24.)

Patterns that work very well are the Corduroy Weave, Swivel Weave, Spot Weaves, M's and O's, and there are many others. Choose your pattern with the following design and structural limitations in mind:
• Because the overshots will be cut to create the standing pile, the height of the pile will be half the length of the overshot.
• The longer the overshot, the more ground weave will be visible between the rows of pile.
• This kind of pile is not dense, since it is limited to the number of shots of weft in the surface pattern.
• A pattern with tabby between pattern shots is necessary, because this builds a firm ground weave and a firm fabric.
• A pattern with long and short overshots can be cut into both long and short pile. Some can be left uncut. Variation is wide.

Color and yarn
Remember that the ground weave and short overshots in the pattern that are not cut are a very visible part of the over-all fabric, so choose compatible colors for warp, pattern weft, and tabby.
You may want to use different shades of one color, or several colors and strong contrast. Three weights of yarn work out well — a heavy, soft yarn for the pile, a medium weight for the warp and a very fine, strong yarn for the tabby.

Design
Blocks of the pattern can be expanded to give you the length overshot desired in the width of the fabric. The warpwise length of the pile rows is determined by the number of weft shots woven in the pattern. The pile rows, when cut, parallel the warps.

Cutting the pile
Floats must be cut very carefully. Blunt-end scissors are preferred.

Swivel and Corduroy
Two subjects from the *Seattle Weavers' Guild Bulletin* were photographed to show you two of the overshot weaves that can be cut for short pile. The swatches were woven and material prepared under the direction of Noel Hammock.

Swivel Weave
This is my kind of backwards approach to a pile weave. The

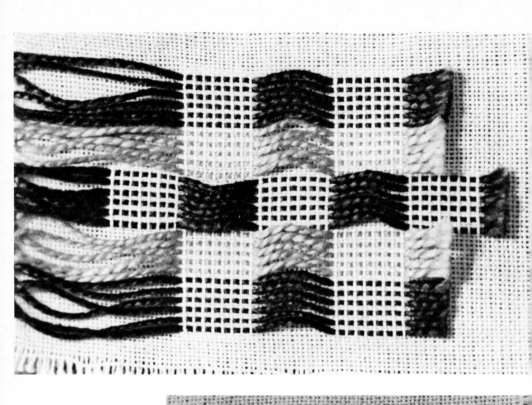

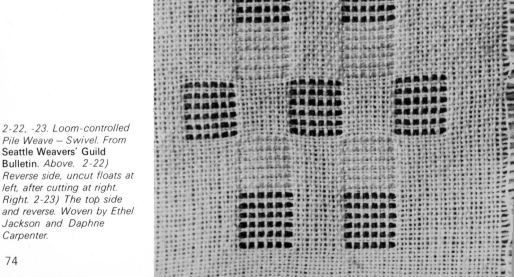

2-22, -23. Loom-controlled Pile Weave — Swivel. From **Seattle Weavers' Guild Bulletin**. *Above. 2-22) Reverse side, uncut floats at left, after cutting at right. Right. 2-23) The top side and reverse. Woven by Ethel Jackson and Daphne Carpenter.*

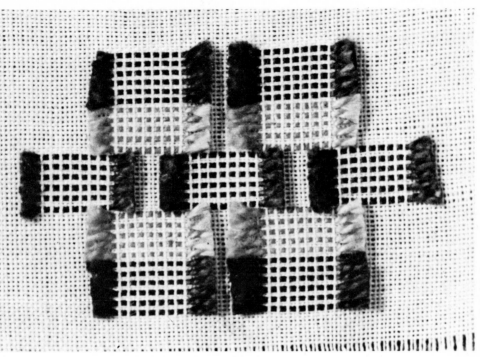

2-24. Corduroy Weave — a loom-controlled pile weave. From the **Seattle Weavers' Guild Bulletin**. By Noel Hammock.

"down-side" showed a charming little fringe along the ends of the squares, and caught our pile-weaving eye. It suggested an interesting way to do a very subtle pile-weave accent. Swivel Weave is a term used by some weavers for certain ways of weaving spot and overshot weaves. The pattern areas are surrounded and divided by plain weave ground.

Corduroy Weave

A good arrangement of overshots to be snipped for pile is provided by this technique. The pile will be in rows, parallel to the warp, and only as dense as your rows of overshot pattern. It is all weaving — no knots — and a fast way to make a good pile fabric. For rugs, with six or more strands of Persian rug wool used as one weft, yarn is greedily used up, but a quickly-made handsome thick pile rug is yours in a few hours. Corduroy can be threaded to have overshots on both top and reverse sides, so you can make a two-faced pile cloth.

More Ideas

Think "surface-interest" and "pile" and keep an open mind when you choose between loom-woven patterns and weaver-controlled methods of raising yarn above the ground weave. You may be surprised at how many techniques can be turned into a fresh new surface-interest weave.

21 Needle-made Pile

Needle-made pile can be done on woven fabric if no loom is available, or desired. Of course, then it is not a handwoven pile but a needlework pile. A well-known method of making traditional Rya rugs is done by inserting Ghiordes Knots made with needle-and-yarn into a background woven with rows of open warp to accommodate the knots. Several embroidery stitches adapt to use for small areas of texture on a flat weave, worked as the weaving progresses. A few inches of the ground weave is finished, then the pile-weave stitch is worked, more flat weave is woven, and so on. Although this method is slow, it is full of inventive possibilities, for accent areas especially, rather than for over-all texture or pile.

2-25. Needle-made Pile Stitches — Sorbello Stitch in several sizes, worked in soft spun wool on a handwoven ground.

Our suggestions are for utilizing embroidery stitches in a different way, enlarging and exaggerating them for a full pile weave but retaining the technique of the stitch, having chosen one that will make a raised surface. See the bibliography for several excellent books on stitches; investigate the methods of doing those we have mentioned here, used and found good for the purpose. You will discover others.

The Sorbello Stitch

Traditionally used in Sorbello, Italy, for embroideries. Makes a raised, puffy surface. (Sorbello will be found in Jacqueline Enthoven's *The Stitches of Creative Embroidery*.) We find uses for this stitch over and over again, when worked with multiple strands of wool in a greatly increased scale — as much as one inch per stitch. (Figure 2-25.) Essentially, the stitch is composed of buttonhole stitches worked on a horizontal bar, and caught at the lower corners. We have used it with success in sizes from one-fourth inch up to nearly two inches.

2-26. Chain Stitch worked in layers for a raised surface, and in several sizes. On handwoven wool background.

Other stitches

Other embroidery stitches that suggest use for a pile surface on a flat-weave ground:

French Knots. These are a surface stitch and stand up from the background. Exaggerated, they became important standing pile. Work them in various sizes, tightly clustered and/or scattered.

Layered stitches. Work Herringbone Stitch in layers, beginning with a tight, narrow row, then over and over this row in ever-widening rows, each in a different color. Carefully cut through the center of the stack of stitches — you will have a rich, thick strip of cut pile. Color selection is a challenge in this method, and a delight. Again, a bit slow, so perhaps best to limit it to small areas of pattern.

Many stitches lend themselves to layering, and it may be an approach to a raised surface that you have not thought of. In figure 2-26 the design problem was to use mainly just one kind of stitch, and enlarge it, layer it, and try new ways of using it. Our example is all chain stitch, some worked over and over to form a raised oval.

In a week-long workshop with Constance Howard, author,

2-27, overleaf, 2-28. Stitchery experiments with yarns and unspun wool, to achieve surface interest. On handwoven raw-silk fabric.

2-28

teacher, and noted stitchery expert, head of The School of Art, Goldsmiths' College, University of London, England, we were inspired to experiment with yarns and stitches to create three-dimensional effects. Figures 2-27 and 2-28 show some of the sampling we did in this direction. Using unspun wool on a handwoven raw-silk fabric, plus various yarns and stitches, resulted in some exciting surface interest — and some that could be called pile surfaces. We show these to give you another idea to pursue.

Couching done in huge scale with any of the suitable couching stitches, from plain overcast to elaborate loop and detached stitches, offers engaging possibilities for a raised surface. Explore the embroidery stitches — you will find many that relate to a pile surface. Look up some of the following, and more: Coxcomb, Berlin Pile, Candlewick, Bullion, Colcha Stitch, the various knotted and detached stitches. Pile weaves can rise from the needle as well as from the loom.

22 Natural Pile Weaves

Wefts from growing things

Wefts from flora and fauna are everywhere in the world around us, waiting to be discovered and woven-in for still different fabric faces.

In Hawaii, the abundant varieties of durable and decorative pods, stems, and leaves offer interesting textures to add to woven textiles. Ruthadell Anderson, Honolulu, produces beautifully designed and crafted weavings, mostly on a large scale, such as those that grace the new Capitol building in Honolulu and Honolulu hotels and banks. She employs woven-pile methods with added textures from nature: Figure 2-29 shows one section from a series of tapestries made for the Honolulu Academy of Arts. (Also see figure 1-6.)

Feathers

Lin Lipetz Longpre, talented weaver and teacher, adds feathers to wrapped warps for texture and interest. (Figure 2-30.)

Gloria Crouse sent a four-sided weaving soaring up over nine feet, with top section of unwoven warp, a hollow square of white loops and feathers for interest at eye-level. (Figure 2-31.)

Fur

Mother Nature is an expert fabricator of pile surfaces! Early-day weavers no doubt observed that animal pelts were composed of strands standing at right angles to the background. Perhaps as a supplement to the furry skins that clothed them, perhaps as a challenge to simulate them in weaving, pile weaves were created. Tags of hair or wool were simply laid into the ground weave and then, to keep them in place, the fabric was soaked and felted. Later, ways to wrap and knot the extra wefts were devised. In very cold areas, the warm, woolly side was used as the inside of coats and covers. Floor coverings and decorative uses of pile weaves came along as sophistication in uses and design evolved. Guatemalan weavers use a low picked-up loop that resembles sheep wool (*Chivas*, figure 2-8); the Icelandic pile fabric (figures 2-10, -11, -12) was made with matted tags of wool put into the ground weave, and looked like a shaggy fleece.

Weaving with fur strips

Today weavers are cutting fur into strips and weaving pile weaves with a pile weft! For our day this makes some sense, since it not only utilizes furs that have seen their best days as apparel, throws, or rugs, but creates textiles that are lush, flexible, and beautiful.

Bonny Cook, who makes a specialty of weaving with fur, provided us with photographs of some of her lovely work. (Figures 1-9, 2-33.) She has written a small book — *Weaving with Antique* Fur (*Second Hand)*, which details the procedures with pictures of handsome woven examples.

Overleaf, 2-29. Detail of large tapestry shown in figure 1-6. Weaver, Ruthadell Anderson. (Photograph by Raymond M. Sato.)

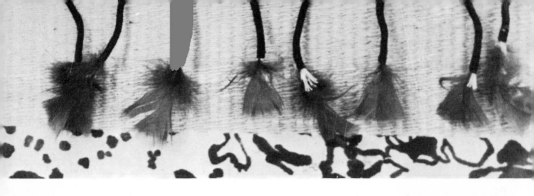

Above, 2-30. Feather-tips on wrapped warps. Woven by Lin Lipetz Longpre, Director, the Factory of Visual Art, Seattle.

Below and right, 2-31. **Albatron**. A hanging nine and one-half feet high White loops and feathers. Detail inset shows the lower section. Woven by Gloria Crouse. (Photograph by Gloria Crouse.)

2-32. **Lopi**. *The pelt of the Iceland mountain sheep, and the wool. Multi-level weaving in Icelandic Cut Pile. (Shown in color on page 21.)*

2-33. "Furniture rug" of white fur strips woven with white wool. Pillow from a fox coat-collar. Weaver, Bonny Cook. (Photograph by Ron De Nend.)

2-34. Pillow of corduroy, with bear fur, needle-made loops, and padded leather. By Fritzi Oxley. (Photograph by Beverly Rush.)

Fritzi Oxley combined shaggy bear fur with needlemade loops on a pillow. (Figure 2-34.)

Fur strips are a rich accent — an instant pile surface — added to pillows, purses, wall hangings, trims, and bands. Wherever a weaver needs a luxurious effect, fur is one good answer. (Figures 2-32-33-34, C-3, C-4).

Design inspiration from nature

For design inspiration just look about and see some of the possibilities in the landscape. Find pile-weave ideas in a row of trees silhouetted against the sky, a hedgerow, bubbling looping surf against sand, a dense coral reef surrounded by low rippling water, a bluejay's crest, a cat's whiskers! Ruffs, tassels, dense standing pile, and soft smoothed-down pile-weave effects are present everywhere. Also be inspired by nature's colors. You will notice

2-35, -36. The natural pile — the woven pile. Below, 2-35) Red-maple branch in bloom. Overleaf, 2-36) Wrapped tassels in unspun wool.

2-36

2-37

in a dandelion bloom, for instance, that many shades of yellow are combined. A silvery pussywillow catkin IS pile-weave in its construction: composed of gray and brown and gold, with an underlay ground "weave" of golden brown. Much as in dyeing yarn with successive, different color dyebaths to achieve a rich, jewel-tone, you will discover that pile-fabric colorings can be built up from an underlying base color that is quite different from the over-all surface colors, and this build-up gives an opulent depth to your weaving. You will find clues for adding many shades of weft in each pile wrap or knot. We have assembled some comparative photographs, showing growing pile along with woven pile weaves that are related in texture, designed to suggest those in nature. Do use the wealth of design and color inspiration all about us. (Figures 1-4, 1-5 and 2-35 — 2-39.)

2-37, 38, -39. A trio of look-alikes. Opposite, below, 2-37) The growing weft on a pine branch. Above, 2-38) An edge view of soft wool pile woven by the author. Overleaf, 2-39) Wiry linen, woven by Lin Lipetz Longpre.

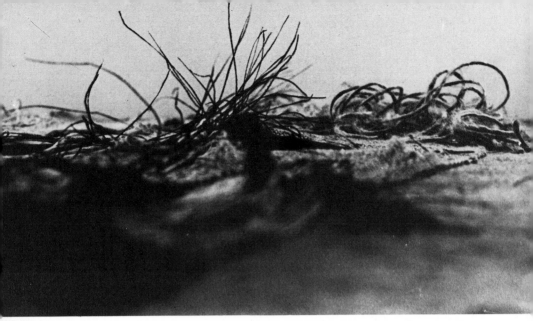

2-39

23, 24, 25, 26 Edges, Ends, and a Joining

The three weft-protector edge finishes we have space left to suggest are just a small patch on the many ways to make a good, secure warp-end finish. These are especially fine for rug edges, which *must* be well done. Follow the yarn path in the drawings.

Wrapped and woven (D-24A, B)

A simple, uncomplicated way to make sure that your fabric will not come unwoven. Each warp in succession is wrapped around the adjoining warp and woven over-and-under successive warps until it is used up. Bring the end up; these ends can be clipped close later. Repeat all the way across. You will have a woven border. (D-24A.) This works even with fairly short warps that weave over and under just a few times, with no wrap. (D-24B.)

D-24. Woven-warp weft-protector edge finishes.
A. Wrapped and woven.
B. Simple over-and-under.

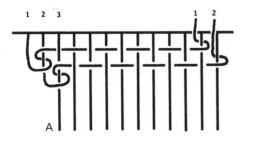

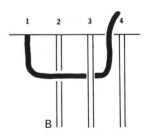

Czech Edge (D-25)

Each warp loops around the adjacent warp, and the end is pulled down. The loop is snugged up to the edge of the cloth. This finish gives a hanging fringe, which can then be further knotted, braided or wrapped. Or it is a good edge left with straight fringe.

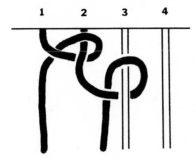

D-25. Czech wrapped edge finish.

Twined Edge (D-26A, B, C)

Twining the warps results in a ridged edge that will hold well. No ends are left hanging. This might be a good choice if your warp is undistinguished and you want to add other yarns for a fringe.

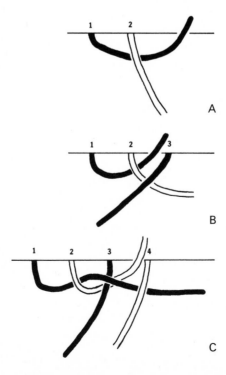

D-26. A, B, C. Twined edge finish — weft protector.

Warp Protectors

Sometimes the warp ends need to be protected to keep them from fraying or tangling when left in a straight fringe. The warp ends can be wrapped — a few at a time. They can be plaited or braided, knotted in a variety of ways. More fringe can be added, then all of it made more decorative by some extra treatment.

Decorative Selvedges

Wefts can be extended out beyond the selvedges to make a weft fringe. Extra wefts can be carried up along the edges as weaving progresses, and woven in and out to form scallops or loops on the selvedge. When you weave in extra rows to build up and strengthen the spaces left by rows of heavy knots, this weft can be a different color and/or yarn, and added in a simple sequence of stripes, squares, triangles. Sometimes just different colors in the selvedge will add a touch to the sides of a textile. When you are weaving chained rows, bring some of the chain out at the selvedge before returning in the opposite direction and make a chained loop or knob. These are all things a weaver can do to lift a textile into a really hand-crafted object. (See figure 1-12.)

A Joining

A "built-in" kind of planned joining of two handwoven pieces is tying warp-ends or weft fringe together. Our little pillow shown in figure 2-40 was part of an experimental weaving. On a frame loom, we wove two separate triangular-shaped pieces at the same time. The triangles were wrapped around a square pillow-form. The weft ends — each colorful weft stripe had been woven in with the ends left hanging — were tied in a simple overhand knot. A diagonal line of "pile" decorates the pillow. The two open sides were sewn together invisibly with matching yarn. Fascinating possibilities here for joining either with the warp ends or the wefts — elaborate or simple knotting. (Also see figures 1-8 and 2-21.)

Opposite, 2-40. Detail of joining on Greek Soumak pillow. The weft ends are tied together.

*Pile weaves are for craftsmen and designers — practical, fanciful, or both. The techniques are wide open for inventive application. Surely some of our fascination and love-affair with the array of pile weaves **must** come through to you! Have a happy, productive time with them.*

Jean Wilson
Bellevue, Washington

Bibliography

New books on weaving and reprints of old ones appear
constantly; keep checking your library, your book store, and
book lists. The books named below are only a few of the many
I have found helpful. Each one has a reference list worth
consulting.

Birrell, Verla. *The Textile Arts: A Handbook of Fabric Structure
and Design Processes.* New York; Harper and Row, 1959.

Collingwood, Peter. *The Techniques of Rug Weaving.* New York;
Watson-Guptil Publications, 1968.

Cook, Bonny. *Weaving with Antique* Fur (*Second hand).*
Bainbridge Island, Washington; Rt. 7, Box 7843, 98110.

D'Harcourt, Raoul. *Textiles of Ancient Peru and their Techniques.*
Translated by Sadie Brown. Edited by Grace G. Denny and
Carolyn Osborn. Seattle; University of Washington Press, 1962.

Dillmont, Therese. *The Encyclopedia of Needlework.* France;
Mulhouse.

Emery, Irene. *The Primary Structures of Fabrics.* Washington, D.C.;
The Textile Museum, 1966.

Enthoven, Jacqueline. *The Stitches of Creative Embroidery.*
New York; Van Nostrand Reinhold, 1964.

————. *Stitchery for Children.* New York; Van Nostrand Reinhold,
1968.

————. *Scroll of Stitches.* New York; Van Nostrand Reinhold,
1972.

Howard, Constance. *Inspiration for Embroidery.* London;
B. T. Batsford Ltd.

Justema, William and Doris. *Weaving & Needlecraft Color
Course.* New York; Van Nostrand Reinhold, 1970.

King, William A. *Warp and Weft from Tibet.* McMinnville,
Oregon; Robin and Russ Handweavers, 533 North Adams Street.
Second printing, 1965.

O'Neale, Lila M. *Textiles of Highland Guatemala* (Publication
No. 567). Washington, D.C.; Carnegie Institution, 1945.

Regensteiner, Else. *The Art of Weaving.* New York: Van Nostrand
Reinhold, 1971.

Tod, Del Deo. *Rug Weaving for Everyone.* (For Corduroy Weave
and Boutonné). New York; Bramhall House.

Wilson, Jean. *Weaving is for Anyone.* New York; Van Nostrand Reinhold, 1967.

——— *Weaving is fun.* New York; Van Nostrand Reinhold, 1971.

———. *Weaving is Creative.* New York; Van Nostrand Reinhold, 1973.

———. *The Pile Weaves.* New York; Van Nostrand Reinhold, 1974.

———. *Weaving you can wear.* New York; Van Nostrand Reinhold, 1974.

Periodicals

Handweaver and Craftsman. 220 Fifth Avenue, New York, N.Y., 10001.

Shuttle, Spindle and Dyepot. Magazine of the Handweavers Guild of America, 339 N. Steele Road, West Hartford, Connecticut, 06117.